THINKING

ABOUT

GOD

BY ALEX EARLY

THEOLOGY Q&A
for KIDS

illustrated by
NATE FARRO

B&H
kids
Brentwood TN

To Tovah and Jude.
You are the joy of my life and my heart's
happiness. I treasure you, respect you,
learn from you, and love you
("with all God's bunches").

Copyright © 2023 by Alex Early
Illustrations by Nate Farro
Illustrations copyright © 2023 by B&H Publishing Group
Published by B&H Publishing Group, Brentwood, Tennessee
All rights reserved
978-1-0877-7139-7
Dewey Decimal Classification: C230
Subject Heading: GOD \ THEOLOGY \ CHRISTIANITY

Unless otherwise noted, Scripture quotations are taken from the Christian Standard Bible®,
Copyright © 2017 by Holman Bible Publishers. Used by permission. Christian Standard Bible®
and CSB® are federally registered trademarks of Holman Bible Publishers.
Scriptures marked ESV are taken from The Holy Bible, English Standard Version®
Copyright © 2001 by Crossway Bibles, a publishing ministry of Good News Publishers.
Scriptures marked NIV are taken from the Holy Bible, New International Version®,
NIV® Copyright ©1973, 1978, 1984, 2011 by Biblica, Inc. Used by permission.
All rights reserved worldwide.
Scriptures marked NKJV are taken from the New King James Version®.
Copyright © 1982 by Thomas Nelson. Used by permission. All rights reserved.
Scriptures marked MSG are taken from The Message.
Copyright © 1993, 2002, 2018 by Eugene H. Peterson.

Printed in Dongguan, Guangdong, China, February 2023
1 2 3 4 5 6 7 • 27 26 25 24 23

CONTENTS

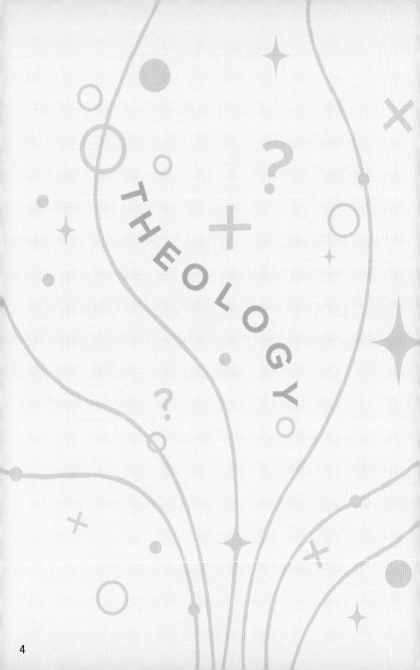

THEOLOGY

THINKING ABOUT THINKING ABOUT GOD

Theology? What's that? Well, theology is the curious, serious, adventuresome, jaw-dropping, mind-blowing study of God. The word *theology* is a combination of two Greek words: *theos*, meaning "God," and *logos*, meaning "word," "reason," or "logic." Theology is thinking about God. Who is He? How has He shown us what He's like? And how does knowing God change the way we think and live?

If this is your first time entering the world of theology, it might sound like something just for grown-ups. You might be a bit nervous or uncomfortable. But I'm opening the door and giving you the warmest, kindest, happiest, and gentlest welcome. You belong here! You are capable of learning about theology, and your brilliant mind, fantastic imagination, and curious questions can feel right at home. In the Bible the apostle Paul encouraged Timothy to continue studying God's Word and to be a leader in the church even while young (1 Timothy 4:12).

Now, theology will stretch your mind, challenge your life, and teach you truths of eternal importance. Theology is serious because God takes His Word, creation, and you very seriously. So come right on in and join people like Abraham, Sarah, Noah, Moses, Miriam, David, Jesus, Mary, Paul, Phoebe, and all the theologians who have been thinking about God all along!

When you think about God, what comes to mind? Do you picture Him making this entire fantastic universe, from the moon to the animals to the people? Maybe mountains and oceans or deserts and rain forests come to mind. Perhaps you think of something tiny like a roly-poly bug or something massive like a redwood tree. Maybe you think about Jesus. Or perhaps you're not sure what to think. Hopefully the questions and answers in this book will fill your mind with amazing things about God!

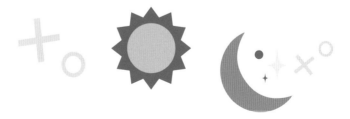

Thinking and Living

God cares a lot about all those thoughts in your head. Why? Well, the things, people, and stories you think about shape the way you live your life. For example, if you fill your thoughts with sports, you'll find yourself wanting to play those sports with friends. If you often wonder about animals, you'll be concerned with how animals are treated. If you think a lot about music, you'll be excited to go to concerts or listen to new songs. So . . . if you think about God a lot, you'll want to live for Him each and every day.

When God created Adam and Eve in His image, He gave them the unique and wonderful ability to think. They could look around the garden of Eden and make decisions that glorified God and helped each other, or they could choose the opposite. (This is what the Bible calls *sin*, and we'll get to that later.) God has given you a mind, and how you use it matters tremendously! Jesus once said, "Love the Lord your God with all your heart, with all your soul, and with all your *mind*" (Matthew 22:37). Loving God with all your mind means using your creative thoughts to bring about God's good in God's world.

In the Bible's book of Proverbs, wise King Solomon said people who think only about the moment and not about God are "foolish." They make choices that seem fun or satisfying but end in disaster. For example, eating a steady diet of only candy might sound fun, but your body won't feel good after a while. It needs healthy vitamins and nutrients. Solomon said the way a person thinks is who he or she really is (Proverbs 23:7 NKJV). Our thoughts eventually become how we behave. Jesus said, "For the mouth speaks from the overflow of the heart" (Matthew 12:34). Our *outward* words and actions reflect the *inward* thoughts of our minds.

The Big Story of the Bible

The best way to begin using our minds to glorify God is to flood our thoughts with the Bible because the Bible is God's story. God wrote the Bible in a way nobody had written a story before or has since: it was written over many, many years with many people writing God's words—but it's all one big story. When I say "big story," I mean the *whole* story of the entire Bible from the very beginning to the very end, Genesis to Revelation. Thinking of the Bible this way is called "biblical theology."

But you might think, *The Bible is super long, with so much going on! How could God be telling just one story?* Well, my friend Jesse once taught me how to tell a story. He said to fill in these blanks:

Once upon a time _____.

And every day _____.

Until one day _____.

And because of that _____.

And because of that _____.

Until finally _____.

And from that day on _____.

The Bible's story might be long, but it can follow this method! Here's the story of the Bible:

Once upon a time, God created the universe and filled it with stars and planets, including Earth. He made all we see, and He made the first people, Adam and Eve.

And every day, God spent time with Adam and Eve in a beautiful garden. They had a perfect friendship with Him. God told them they could enjoy anything they wanted in the garden except fruit from the Tree of Knowledge of Good and Evil. If they did, they would be separated from God.

Until one day, Satan, God's enemy, deceived the humans. They ate the fruit—the only thing God had told them *not* to do. God's promise of death (being physically and relationally separated from God) came true. However, before God sent Adam and Eve away, He promised to destroy the serpent (Satan) one day and to make perfect friendship between God and His people again. This is the first announcement of the good news that God would save His creation!

And because of that, sin and death are in the world. Every sad thing happens because of that day, and every person is affected.

And because of that, God sent Jesus to redeem (to save!) the world. Jesus lived a perfect life. He never disobeyed God like Adam and Eve did and every other person has. He died on a cross to pay for the punishment of sin. Then He rose from the dead and returned to heaven to live with His Father, God. Followers of Jesus eagerly await His return.

Until finally, Jesus returns to judge, heal, and restore all of creation so that we can be in perfect friendship with God again.

And from that day on, all will be right again.

What a wonderful story! And every bit of it is real. When God wrote His big story, the Bible, He divided it into four major scenes (kind of like acts in a play!): Creation, Fall, Redemption, and Restoration. Can you see all four scenes in God's story that you just read? God created the world; Adam and Eve sinned and were separated from God; God sent Jesus to redeem the world; and one day Jesus will return to restore all creation.

This is the story the church has read, studied, and tried to live by for thousands of years. God's story is great because it is like God:

God is true, so His story is true.

God is the Creator, so His story is creative.

God is powerful, so His story is powerful.

God is love, so His story is loving.

God is our Savior, so His story tells us about how He saves.

The better we know God's story, the better we are at thinking about Him and living for Him. Throughout your life, many things will change, from where you live and go to school to the kind of life you have as an adult. There will be moments when you couldn't possibly be happier.

There will also be heartbreaking moments because bad and sad things do happen in the world. God's story is there to guide you through every single moment. Even though life changes, God doesn't change, and because God doesn't change, His story remains the same.

So you and I have a lot of thinking to do in this book. I've written it as questions and answers that take you on a bit of a tour around the world of theology. It's fascinating stuff, and it's all about God. We'll discover more about His big story, and we'll think about and wonder at our awesome God together. I'm really glad you're here! You belong.

Alex

THEOLOGY is the curious, serious, adventuresome, jaw-dropping, mind-blowing study of God.

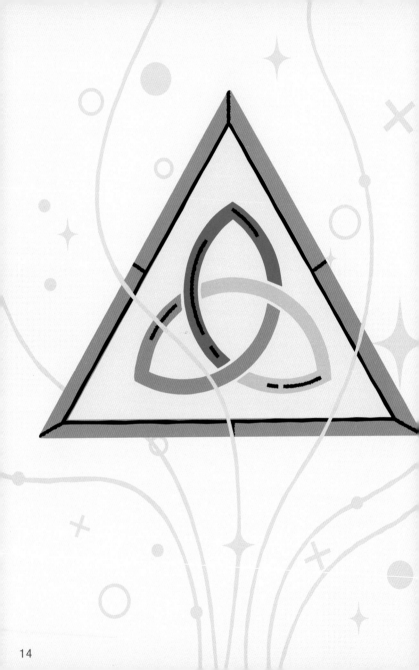

THE TRINITY

The first verse of the Bible says, "In the beginning, God created the heavens and the earth" (Genesis 1:1 ESV). But let's begin *before* the beginning. Let's begin with God. Scripture teaches us God exists as three persons—Father, Son, and Holy Spirit. This is what we call the **Trinity**. It is important to understand God is not a ghost, a force, or an impersonal spirit. God reveals Himself as "Father," which means He must have a child. And He does. The eternal Father has always had a Son. And this Son came to earth in the person of Jesus Christ. Jesus brings other people into a relationship with God the Father so that God can have lots and lots of kids, and we can all have the best Father imaginable. The Holy Spirit is the third person of the Trinity.

God exists as THREE persons— Father, Son, and Holy Spirit.

He is the One who binds the Father and the Son together in love and who binds us together with the Father, reminding us all the time that we are God's children.

Where does the word *TRINITY* come from?

Fun fact: the word *Trinity* never appears in the Bible. It's a word Christians use to describe something that is taught in the Bible—that our one God is three persons. The first time we know of the word being used was almost two hundred years after Jesus lived on earth! A man named Theophilus wrote the word (in Greek) in a letter to a friend. About twenty years after that, a man named Tertullian (yes, his name sounds like the cute shell-backed reptiles!) also used the word *Trinity* to describe God the Father, God the Son, and God the Holy Spirit. Only this time, Tertullian wasn't speaking with a friend. He was in a huge public debate with people who disagreed with him about God. Tertullian was from the country of Tunisia, which is in North Africa. Instead of speaking Greek, Tertullian spoke Latin. So in a way, Theophilus and Tertullian both used the word *Trinity* first.

Who are the members of the Trinity?

Throughout Scripture (the Bible), we learn God is one being in three persons. The Father is God; the Son is God; the Holy Spirit is God. Paul said of the Father, "Yet for us there is one God, the Father, from whom are all things and for whom we exist, and one Lord, Jesus Christ, through whom are all things and through whom we exist" (1 Corinthians 8:6 ESV). Jesus said of Himself, "I and the Father are one" (John 10:30 ESV). Finally, Jesus said of the Holy Spirit, "I tell you the truth: it is to your advantage that I go away, for if I do not go away, the Helper will not come to you. But if I go, I will send him to you" (John 16:7 ESV).

So, are there three Gods or one?

Our *one* God exists as *three* persons. Probably nothing is more complicated to understand than that sentence! How can God be one and three at the same time?

Although many writers and scholars have tried to come up with complete ways to describe the one-ness and three-ness of God, nobody can. Not me, not your parents or Sunday school teacher, not even the smartest people ever! Every metaphor falls short.

For example, some people will say, "God is like H2O. It can be ice, water, or steam, and it's still all made of the same H2O molecules." Even though this idea is clever, it doesn't work. The same H2O molecules cannot be ice, steam, and water all at the same time. They must change. But God does not change. He is all three persons (Father, Son, Spirit) at once, always.

No human can really grasp how the Trinity is possible. Why? Nothing else in creation is like God! God was not made in a factory somewhere. He has always existed as one and three. This is known as the doctrine (which means teaching) of **aseity**. Nobody *made* God! God is a perfect, loving, glorifying, creative relationship. In chapter 3 we'll learn all creation exists as an *overflow* of the love shared within the Trinity.

God not only has relationships between the Father, Son, and Holy Spirit, but He also has relationships with every person who trusts in Jesus. Prayer is one way we build that relationship with God. Think about your closest friends. To keep those relationships strong, you need to spend time with those friends, talking with them and listening to them. Prayer is similar! It is spending time with the Trinity, talking and listening.

You can pray to the Father, Son, or Holy Spirit. Our prayers are heard by God the Father because of Jesus's sacrifice and with the Holy Spirit's help. So, we pray *to* the Father, *through* the Son, *by* the Holy Spirit. If you are a Christian, God the Holy Spirit is always with you. In fact, the Spirit stays in relationship with you and helps you pray to the Father and Jesus. Because God is one being in three persons, each member of the Trinity is listening to you, loving you, and ready to guide you when you pray.

TO **THINK** ABOUT:

When you begin to understand that God Himself is a relationship, how does that make you think differently about the importance of your relationships?

How can you better connect with God, your church, or your friends and family?

Do strong, healthy connections with other humans help your relationship with God?

We pray
to the FATHER,
through the SON,
by the HOLY
SPIRIT.

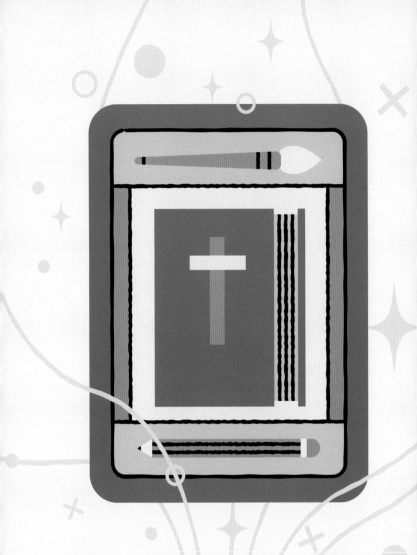

GOD

You might have wondered, *What is God like? Does He ever sleep? Does He ever mess up or fail?* We find answers to those questions in the **attributes** of God. Attributes are qualities or characteristics that describe someone. We might say artists are creative, soccer players are fast, and gymnasts are flexible. Those are their attributes. The Father, Son, and Holy Spirit also all have attributes that describe what God is like.

We learn about God's attributes through creation and through the Bible. Paul said God's "invisible attributes, that is, his eternal power and divine nature, have been clearly seen since the creation of the world, being understood through what he has made" (Romans 1:20). In other words, as we look at God's beautiful creation all around us—mountains,

> We learn about GOD's attributes through creation and through the Bible.

trees, stars, oceans, animals—we know some things about God: He is perfect and consistent in all that He is and does, and His power is limitless. Looking around at nature and learning about God is called general revelation. God has *revealed* or *shown* these things about Himself to people all over the world.

Yet there's a revelation even better, even more special. We have the Bible! Second Timothy 3:16 says the Bible is the *words* of God! This is called special revelation. Being able to hold and read God's words on a page is special, right? As we read the Bible, we don't read about God's favorite color or song; we read about the most important things we need to know about Him. So, let's think and learn about what God is like. How is He different from us? How is He like us?

How is God different from us?

God is the perfect, eternal Trinity, and He is the Creator of all things. God is different from us in tons of other ways too!

Some of His attributes are unique to Him. Nothing else in creation—no humans, angels, or animals—is like God in these ways. These attributes are called **incommunicable**. It's a long word, but it just means that people don't have these same attributes—not even the tiniest amount. Try saying that word out loud: *in-com-yoon-i-cah-bl*. Here are just three of the important ways God is different from us:

1. **God is omnipresent**, meaning He is everywhere at one time. *Omni* means "all," and *present* means "here." God is everywhere at once. We can only be in one place at a time.

2. **God is omnipotent**, meaning He is all-powerful, more than anything and anyone. God can do literally anything, but we are limited in size and strength.

3. **God is omniscient**, meaning He knows everything. God never has to think hard to remember something or look for the answer to a question. As humans, we often forget or don't understand things, and we always have more to learn.

How is God like us?

God has **communicable** attributes too! He shares or *communicates* some of His characteristics with people. For example, God is perfectly good, and we are capable of goodness. God is relational, and we are relational. God is supremely intelligent, and we can grow in intelligence. Of course, God is all these things perfectly—we are not.

God also shares attributes like being truthful, honorable, loving, holy, patient, wise, and kind with us. When someone is kind toward you, you can remember God is infinitely more kind than the kindest person in the world! As He shares these attributes with us, we get to know more about Him. We know these things because of what He reveals throughout the Bible.

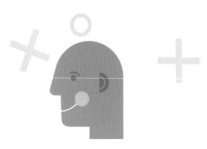

Why is it hard to understand God?

If you try to understand all there is to know about God, you might end up with a headache. But why? It's hard for us to understand God for two reasons. First, the Bible never says God intended Adam and Eve to know everything there is to know about God. He is so big and different from us that it's impossible to know everything there is to know about Him! Second, sin entered creation. It affected everything, including how we think. This is called the **noetic effects of sin**. (We will talk more about sin in chapter 5). The word *noetic* means "mental activity." It refers to our ability to think.

In the garden of Eden, Adam and Eve could understand God and relate to God without any problems or confusion. In the afternoons, they would enjoy their time with God, knowing Him and being known by Him.

But after sin entered the world, everything changed. Death, sadness, and pain hurt all of creation, including the way we think. Now we struggle to believe, trust, and have faith in God. Ultimately, the reason it's hard to understand God is because of sin.

TO THINK ABOUT:

Think about what it might have felt like to be in the garden of Eden, spending time walking around and talking with God. Do you think God enjoyed this time with Adam and Eve? How does He feel when you spend time with Him today?

CREATION

We live in a fast-paced society. Many people don't slow down to think about the world around them. Technology is everywhere. There are schedules to keep, school projects to do, chores that need checking, and practices to attend! Slowing down and paying attention to all that God created is challenging. Let's take a moment to think about the world in which we live.

When the Bible speaks of creation, it refers to everything God made. This includes the universe—the burning sun, the frozen moon, the glimmering stars, and the mysterious planets all hanging quietly in space. When God made Earth, He placed birds in the sky, marine life in the sea, lions in the deserts, penguins on the ice caps, skunks in the forests, alligators in the swamps, and horses in the meadows!

> When the Bible speaks of CREATION, it refers to everything God made.

Fruit and vegetables of every kind spring out of the black soil, growing on vines and trees. Ponds turn into streams, and fresh water rolls down the mountainsides. All this creation is totally alive, buzzing with energy. It all reflects the great creativity of God!

Why did God make everything?

Maybe you wonder, *Why did God make all of this? Was He bored? Did He need something to do or someone to talk to?* God is never bored or lonely, and He never needs anything. God doesn't want to be entertained. He doesn't look for distractions to pass the time. Remember, as the Trinity—Father, Son, and Holy Spirit—God was perfectly content before creating anything, which means creation comes from the overflow of love and inventiveness shared within the Trinity. God created, not because something was "missing," but because that's what artists do—they create!

How did God make everything?

During art class, you follow your teacher's instructions about what to create and use supplies your teacher provides. Your tools might be paper, glue, markers, paint, or clay. When you bring your work home, your parents love to see the results! That's because your artwork is the result of the time, thought, creativity, and skill you used to *create* something. But what about God's artwork—creation? Where did He get His supplies? Who gave Him instructions? Where did He get His inspiration?

God did not need tools or supplies to bring everything into creation. Instead, He did what only He could miraculously do. He made everything from *nothing*. We can't even comprehend that! Theologians use a Latin phrase to describe this mystery: ex nihilo, which means "out of nothing." In the presence of God, nothing becomes something. As human beings, we're far from having that kind of power, but God is omnipotent, remember? He's all-powerful! The Bible says, "God said . . . and God saw" (Genesis 1:3–31). That's how strong God's words are. He speaks, and things appear.

Why should I care about creation?

In Genesis, God told Adam and Eve to rule over the created world (Genesis 1:26–28). They were to work in the garden, come alongside God as co-creators, and tend the earth by pruning, cutting, building, and cultivating more beauty. All of creation belongs to God, so those of us who love God want to take care of His world. As we go about life, we can strive to be good stewards of everything God has made. We can improve the lives of people who come after us by doing things like recycling, finding ways to care for animals, or even starting a garden and growing our own vegetables.

TO THINK ABOUT:

Imagine what it would be like if God had created a world that was entirely dull and dim—no beautiful colors, no glorious sea life or rain forests or sunsets. How would our lives be different? Why do you think God made our world with such beauty?

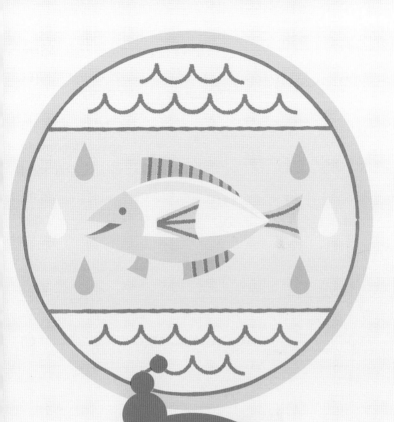

GOD CREATED, not because something was "missing," but because that's what artists do—they create!

HUMANS

The Bible says that after making the land and water and plants and animals and all the things, God wasn't finished. He saved His best work for last. He made **humans**! When we look at people around the world, we see God's creativity on display. We have different skin colors, various eye colors and nose shapes, and unique hair textures. We speak thousands of languages and have different accents. We even enjoy different kinds of food and clothes! All these amazing differences reflect God's creativity, so we celebrate them.

> God saved His best work for last. He made HUMANS!

Why did God create humans?

Before Genesis was written, many religions taught that humans were created by false gods—not the one true God. These ancient legends said humans weren't made because of an overflow of love. We were made as slaves to work for the gods.

But Genesis opens with the opposite story—a story of beauty and creativity and glory! Humans weren't created for slavery and abuse. We were created in the image of God to be loved and live on the earth, working and resting and enjoying each other and our Maker. We were made carefully by God for friendship with Him and each other. As humans, we are unique among everything else God made. We are the only thing in all of creation made in His image (Genesis 1:26–27).

How are humans made in the image of God?

When we think of the word image, we think of a picture or symbol. We think of things we see. So, you may think being made in God's image means we look like what God looks like *physically*, with two arms, two legs, and a nose in the middle of our faces. But being made in God's image actually means we resemble Him in some of our attributes. Think about your shadow. Your shadow is not you. It doesn't look *completely* like you, but it does copy your movements. As humans, we are like little shadows of God, reflecting parts of His character whether we know Him or not.

Do you remember how we discussed the communicable attributes of God? We have some of the characteristics He has, even though we are imperfect in the way we express them. Some examples of God's communicable attributes are goodness, mercy, truthfulness, justice, and grace. When humans practice any of those things, we can see glimmers of how we are made in God's image.

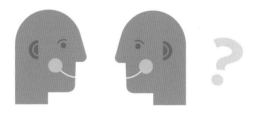

We reflect God in other ways too. Like Him, humans are able to think critically and creatively. We can use our intellect in ways that animals do not. Also, we are moral creatures with a sense of right and wrong. Our consciences tell us whether we should make a certain moral choice or not. Lastly, we are relational, social creatures, which reflects the way God is relational between the Father, Son, and Holy Spirit.

Human beings are precious to God! He made every one of us in His image. There will never be a moment of your life when you are not in the image of God. When God sees you, He sees someone He loves. God values people simply because they are people. His love is not based on whether you get good grades, perform well in a sporting event, have good looks, or have unique talents or abilities. Psalm 139:14 says humans are "remarkably and wondrously made" by God. Therefore, you, your body, and everyone else's body have value, worth, and dignity because we were made by God and for God.

×**?**×

Make a list of three of your positive attributes. Are you kind or funny? Creative or brave? Maybe you're a good listener or a hard worker. Why do you think God gave you those attributes? Do you think they reflect God's image?

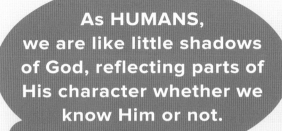

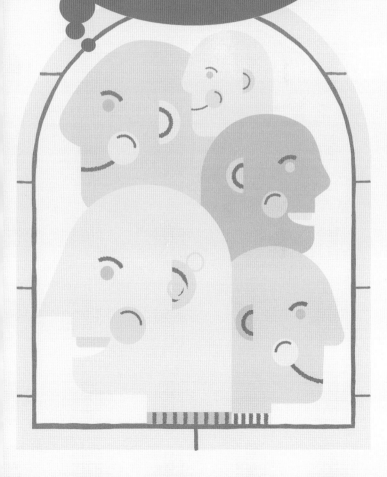

43

SIN

When God made the world, everything was good. There was no evil, fighting, crying, sickness, or death. The world did not need police officers to keep people safe, firefighters to rescue us from disasters, or paramedics to rush people to the hospital. You couldn't find a cemetery because there was no death. That sounds wonderful, doesn't it? That was the world God made and the world He's going to remake one day! All those sad things exist now because of what the Bible calls sin. Sin affects everything. It messes up relationships, makes work difficult, and leads our minds into bad decisions. Even though we humans are made in the image of God, we are all sinful.

Even though we humans are made in the image of God, we are all SINFUL.

What is sin, and where did it come from?

Sin is disobeying God. Any time our thoughts, motives, or actions are not in line with God's desires, we sin. Genesis tells us sin came into the world when the serpent slithered into the garden of Eden and deceived Adam and Eve (Genesis 3:1–7). The serpent tempted them to distrust God and to eat the fruit God had forbidden, saying, "If you eat of the fruit, you will be like God." God warned Adam and Eve that if they ate that fruit, they would die. Still, Eve took the fruit, ate it, and gave it to Adam, who did the same. All the pain of the world begins there.

Why does sin matter so much to God?

At its core, sin breaks relationships between God, yourself, and others. This is why sin matters so much to God. He is holy and loving, and sin rejects holiness and love.

In the garden, Adam and Eve lived in perfect harmony with God, self, and each other. Eve took the fruit because she believed the lying serpent. She believed

God was withholding something good from her, and she was going to see to it that she didn't miss out. She and Adam became sinful by distrusting God, insisting on doing things their own way, and breaking His command. This moment is known as the **Fall** because Adam and Eve *fell* away from obeying God.

After the Fall, people began making bad decisions—and for all the wrong reasons. Today, the world continues to tell us that sin is okay and that selfishness and lying and disobeying God's rules are no big deal. But all sin breaks our relationship with God, and that's definitely a big deal.

Sin offends God, who loves us and made us. Because of sin, we will always fall short of God's standard until Jesus returns and makes everything new again. We need His grace, mercy, and forgiveness to restore our relationship with Him.

Why does
God allow sin,
Satan, and evil
to exist?

This question is ancient and uncomfortable. It's not a question about God's power. We know He can do anything, including putting an end to evil forever. It's a question about God's *character*, right now. Can we say God is always *good* (even right now) as He allows sin, Satan, evil, and all the consequences of a fallen world to exist?

Yes! God is still good. In fact, God only allows sin and evil to go on because He's achieving an even greater purpose. Peter told us God "is restraining himself on account of you, holding back the End because he doesn't want anyone lost. He's giving everyone space and time to change" (2 Peter 3:9 MSG). God will conquer Satan; that's definite. But He allows sin to go on right now because He is patiently working and waiting for the people He loves to believe and follow Him.

TO THINK ABOUT:

Think of a time you hurt a friend's feelings or disobeyed your parents or guardian. How did it make you feel? Did you want to be around them? When you sin, do you feel like God doesn't want to talk with you anymore? Although sin hurts our relationship with God, He most certainly still wants to talk with you!

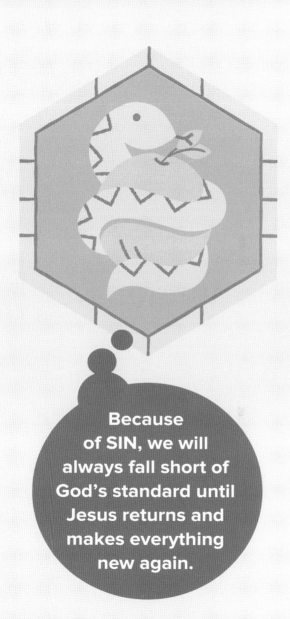

Because of SIN, we will always fall short of God's standard until Jesus returns and makes everything new again.

LEADERS

After creation fell into sin, humans desperately needed leadership. People could no longer walk with God in the garden, free from sin and brokenness. They were unable to trust each other, and they hardly agreed on anything. Leadership was needed, so God provided it. He did not leave His people alone. He gave them different types of leaders. In the Old Testament, those leaders were prophets, priests, and kings.

In the Old Testament, LEADERS were prophets, priests, and kings.

What did prophets, priests, and kings do?

God rescued His people from slavery in Egypt. Eventually, the people settled in a land they called Israel. Throughout Israel's history, the people turned away and worshiped other gods. God sent prophets to be His voice. They spoke messages of repentance and judgment. The prophets were men and women who preached and taught the people about God's law, reminding them how God wanted them to live. Sometimes they would even predict what was going to happen in the future.

The priests were leaders who cared for the temple, offered sacrifices for sins, prayed for the people, and counseled them in God's ways. After the Lord rescued the Israelites (the Hebrews) from slavery in Egypt, He gave Moses the Law.

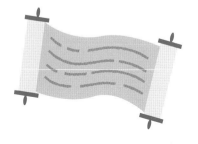

It included the Ten Commandments and many other instructions on how God wanted His people to live together day by day. The priests regularly taught from the Law about what God wanted *from* and *for* His people.

What did God want *from* them? Obedience. What did God want *for* them? Joy. Both things were so clearly God's plan in the garden of Eden.

The kings led the nation and the military. Ideally,

God would be the only king of His people. But the Israelites rejected God as King. They wanted certain men in power (Deuteronomy 17:14). Some of the kings led well, and others failed terribly. The book of Judges teaches us about a long period in Israel's history in which no king ruled over the land: "Everyone did what was right in his own eyes" (Judges 21:25 NKJV).

Societies work best with good leaders who provide peace and justice for everyone. Because sin affected every part of life, God's people needed tremendous help. They needed leaders to serve them in ways that would help them. They needed prophets to proclaim God's Word, priests to help them worship, and kings to rule over them. Yet every prophet, priest, and king failed in one way or another. They all sinned just like every other person who ever lived. They too needed saving! The rescuers needed to be rescued. The helpers needed to be helped. The leaders needed to be led.

The Bible has only one true hero, and it's not any of those human leaders. That hero is Jesus. He is the great Prophet, Priest, and King! As the greatest prophet, Jesus always tells the truth and guides His people toward living in a way that glorifies God. As the greatest priest, Jesus not only listens to and prays for us but also sacrificed His life on the cross to take away our sins. As the truest king, Jesus is the one who will make all things new and lead us to His kingdom, which will have no end. The Gospel of Luke says, "And beginning with Moses and all the Prophets,

he [Jesus] interpreted to them in all the Scriptures the things concerning himself" (Luke 24:27 ESV). Jesus took the time to show the disciples how each story and event throughout the Old Testament pointed to Him.

Do I have to obey leaders, such as my parents?

We might be tempted to think that since Jesus is King, we don't have to obey human leaders in authority. Do we really have to obey our parents, teachers, and police officers? The answer is yes! The fifth commandment says to "honor your father and your mother" (Exodus 20:12). Part of honoring our parents is living in ways that please them. Jesus said, "Give to Caesar the things that are Caesar's, and to God the things that are God's" (Mark 12:17). We are to pay our taxes to the government. Paul said we are to submit to the authorities who are in charge (Romans 13:1–7). Sometimes obeying authorities can be very challenging. Remember that you can pray and ask the Holy Spirit to help you in moments when obedience is the last thing you want to do.

TO **THINK** ABOUT:

Name a few good leaders and a few bad leaders you've known or heard about. Maybe you have a favorite coach or wonderful teacher who comes to mind. What made them a great leader? How can following God make someone a better leader?

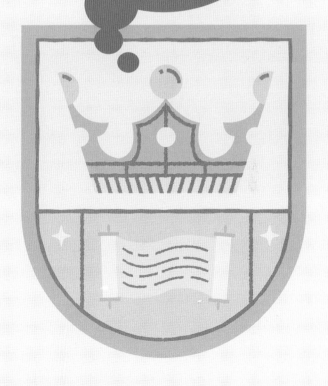

JESUS

You might know that *biology* means the study of living organisms. And *zoology* is the study of animals. But here's a new word for you: **Christology**. *Christ* is the word that means "Messiah," and *ology* is the word we use to describe a particular subject being studied. So *Christology* is the word theologians use to talk about the study of Jesus. *What was He like as a person? What kind of work did He do?* We'll learn a lot more about Jesus (and how He is fully God *and* fully human) in the next few chapters, but this one will explore what Jesus was like, His relationships, and how He connected with people.

CHRISTOLOGY is the word theologians use to talk about the study of Jesus.

When you think of Jesus, what do you imagine He looked like? He was from Israel, so we can assume He had brown skin and dark hair common for men from that part of the world. He was probably strong and had callouses on his hands because He was a carpenter. His daily tools were most likely saws, hammers, nails, and toolboxes as He worked hard day by day in the sunshine.

But what were Jesus's relationships like? He did far more than preach, teach, and heal people. It's important to really understand this because you might think Jesus didn't have friends or didn't take the time to get to know people around Him. He was too important for that, right? Actually, that couldn't be further from the truth! The Gospels tell us much about Jesus's life, ministry, and friendships. He valued people and their needs and reflected His Father's love for them.

What was Jesus like as a kid?

We don't know much about Jesus when He was young. It's easy to wonder what He was like as a boy. *Did He ever fall and hurt Himself? Did He always share with His siblings? Did He have His own bedroom? Did He always keep it clean?* The Gospels teach us that Jesus was 100 percent human, but He was also 100 percent God; therefore, He was perfect. Yes, completely *perfect* in every way and yet totally human. So He probably did fall and skin His knees. Maybe He did need to be told to clean up. But questions like this can be tricky because the Bible doesn't say these things exactly; it's best to move on to what the Bible says clearly. We have a story from when Jesus was twelve years old, and this one story teaches us that young Jesus was intelligent, inquisitive, and a bit adventurous.

Every year, Jesus's family would take a long journey on foot to the city of Jerusalem for a festival called Passover. When the festival was complete, the family would pack up and caravan home with many other people. However, during this particular year, after the first day of the journey back home, they realized Jesus was nowhere to be found! Where had He gone? Was He safe?

Mary and Joseph journeyed back to Jerusalem, searched for *three* days, and finally found Jesus at the temple (the place of worship), where He was asking questions and giving answers to the teachers. Everyone was amazed by how Jesus talked about God! Mary and Joseph told Jesus they had been worried about Him and had looked everywhere. Jesus responded, "Didn't you know I had to be in my Father's house?" (Luke 2:49 NIV). As a middle-school-age boy, Jesus was deeply interested in His Father, God.

Who were Jesus's friends?

The Gospels tell us Jesus had close friends known as His disciples (Matthew 11:1; John 15:15). His three closest friends were Peter, James, and John. These men weren't perfect, but Jesus liked them very much and included them in some of the most fantastic moments of His ministry, like when His body changed on the mountaintop and "His face shone like the sun" (Matthew 17:2 NIV)! (This incredible event is called the transfiguration.)

Jesus also had friends who were not His disciples. In fact, He was known as a friend of sinners (Luke 15:1–2).

This means Jesus didn't wait for people to clean up their act, try hard to be good, and obey all the commandments *before* He was kind to them. Quite the opposite! Jesus shared meals and spent time with people who were far from God. He wanted everyone to know how God loves people and is always pursuing them (see Luke 15). You see, Jesus was acting exactly like His Father. He once said God "is kind to the ungrateful and the evil" (Luke 6:35 ESV).

Why did Jesus perform miracles that helped people?

Not only was Jesus friends with all kinds of people, but He also cared deeply about unpopular, needy people who were often overlooked by everyone else. He worked countless miracles to feed the hungry, heal the sick, and provide for the poor. Jesus taught that feeding hungry people, giving thirsty people something to drink, providing clothing for people in need, caring for sick people, and welcoming strangers were all extremely important. He even said, "Whatever you did for one of the least of these brothers and sisters of mine, you did for me" (Matthew 25:40).

Jesus also had a very special place in His heart for those with physical disabilities, people who had issues or illnesses that made it hard for them to move around, work, or play. Think about when Jesus healed a deaf man. Suddenly the man could hear a friend say hello and hear his family sing on his birthday! Or read the wonderful stories in the Gospels where Jesus healed people who were unable to walk. He could walk right up and simply say, "Get up . . . pick up your mat and walk," and they would walk (John 5:8)! Their bodies would be healed and strengthened, and they would be completely restored. Can you imagine how happy they were to be made well?

When Jesus gave sight to people who were blind, He wanted them to see all God had made—animals, mountains, lakes, the sky, and the colors that make our world so wonderful. More than that, Jesus healed the blind and worked His miracles to create faith in the people being healed as well as those watching Him do the impossible. He showed that He is God and longs to have a relationship with people.

Jesus's miracles serve as road signs, letting us know what's coming up ahead. This means that every time you see a miracle in the Gospels, that's Jesus's way of saying, "This is what the world is going to look like everywhere when I return. No more hungry people. No more sick people. No more lonely people. No more bullies. In my world, everyone is happy and whole. Everyone belongs."

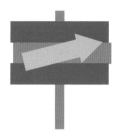

Does Jesus like kids?

Yes! Jesus really likes kids! The Gospels tell us one story in which Jesus was picking children up in His arms, holding them, blessing them, listening to them, and encouraging them (Matthew 19:13–15). Some of the disciples disapproved, thinking Jesus should be spending His time with those they thought were "important people"—the rich or powerful. But Jesus didn't respect that kind of thinking at all. He loved being around children because their soft hearts eagerly believed and trusted Him!

TO **THINK** ABOUT:

What are three ways you have been like Jesus this week? Did you make friends with someone who was left out or rejected? Did you take the time to encourage someone and build them up?

How were you unlike Jesus? Perhaps you struggled to obey your parents. Maybe you didn't share with a sibling. What are some things you can do tomorrow to be more like Jesus?

The Gospels tell us that JESUS valued people and their needs and reflected His Father's love for them.

THE ATONEMENT

Christianity is unique among all the world's religions, starting with the symbol often used to represent it— the cross. The Islamic religion uses an image of a crescent moon and star to symbolize guidance through life. Buddhism uses the dharma wheel to symbolize ongoing spiritual change. Judaism uses the Star of David to represent God's protection of His people. But the symbol of Christianity is the cross, something used for torture and death. How strange!

Jesus was betrayed by His friend Judas. He was beaten, mocked, and spit on by the Romans. Then, because of the Jewish authorities, He suffered death by being crucified on a cross.

> The symbol of Christianity is the CROSS, something used for torture and death. How strange!

The perfect, loving, kind, forgiving Lord Jesus was put to a shameful and painful death. You might wonder, *What did Jesus do to deserve to be treated this way? Where was God the Father when Jesus was put to death? Why didn't He stop it from happening?* The theological word used to answer these questions is atonement, which means "to cover." God knew our sins needed to be covered so we could have a relationship with Him.

The religious leaders of the day hated Jesus because He kept saying He was God (John 8:58). In those times, claiming to be God was punishable by death. Jesus never stopped talking about being the Son of God the Father, which made the religious leaders angrier. *Certainly, nobody walking around in human flesh from a little town like Nazareth could actually be the Son of God!* they thought. Yet it was true. Jesus wasn't lying! He really was the Son of God! Even though His teaching and many miracles offered proof (John 5:36), the authorities didn't believe Him, so they put Him to death.

But Jesus and His Father had a plan. They were working *together*. What were they up to? The Bible teaches us that when Jesus died, He died in our place, causing the judgment of God to pass over His people (1 Corinthians 5:7). His sacrifice covered us. That's the work of atonement.

What's a Passover lamb?

When learning about atonement, the Bible gives us the backstory in the book of Exodus; most importantly, we learn about the Passover lamb. God's people (the Hebrews) were held in captivity in Egypt and were forced to work as slaves for Pharaoh. They had to work very hard all day long every day of their lives. No breaks. No vacations. No time to relax. They were forced to build a giant palace for Pharaoh. This went on for more than four hundred years!

The people cried out to God, saying, "Please rescue us!" God heard their prayers and chose a man named Moses to lead the people out of Egypt. He told Moses to tell Pharaoh, "Let my people go, so that they may worship me" (Exodus 8:1). Each time Moses delivered the message, Pharaoh refused, and God sent a plague—a disaster such as the river turning to blood, frogs filling the land, or fire and ice falling from the sky.

But for the *tenth* plague, God promised to send an angel of death to go through Egypt and kill the firstborn in each family. To save Hebrew families from this plague, God told His people to sacrifice (to offer through death) a lamb, put the lamb's blood on their doorposts, and then go inside. The people obeyed. When God saw this sign on the doorposts of the Hebrews, He caused the angel of death to *pass over* the home, and no one inside was hurt (Exodus 12:13). So although the people were guilty of sin and needed atonement, they were *covered* by the blood of the lamb. They were *rescued*!

The Egyptians did not use the blood of these "pass over" lambs and were not covered. After seeing the loss from the tenth plague, Pharaoh let God's people go.

Why did Jesus die?

When Jesus died on the cross, His death as the Lamb of God served much like the Passover lamb's death long ago. His perfect blood covers the people of God. Understanding the death of Jesus this way is so important because it answers the question "How can God have a relationship with sinful people like you and me?" God never stopped being completely holy and just. Because He sees the blood of Jesus as our substitute, He is able to love us and have a relationship with us while remaining perfectly holy.

This aspect of atonement is called **propitiation**, a big word used in several places in the New Testament. For example, John wrote, "He is the propitiation for our sins, and not for ours only but also for the sins of the whole world" (1 John 2:2 ESV). This means we deserve to be judged for our sins. Yet because Jesus died as our substitute, God's judgment is satisfied, and it passes over us while God's love flows to us.

Because Jesus's death causes God's judgment to pass over us, does that mean God was mad at Jesus?

The answer is no! As we talk about Jesus dying for our sins, one extremely important thing to remember is that He is a member of the Trinity, so He perfectly cooperates with the Father and Holy Spirit. Jesus repeatedly said things like "I and the Father are one" (John 10:30). He also said, "This is why the Father loves me, because I lay down my life so that I may take it up again. No one takes it from me, but I lay it down on my own. I have the right to lay it down, and I have the right to take it up again" (John 10:17–18). Jesus was not forced to die for our sins; He chose to die for us.

TO THINK ABOUT:

The Hebrews had to sacrifice (offer) a lamb. Jesus sacrificed Himself. Can you think of ways you or your family makes sacrifices today? Do your parents give up their time or money for people who need help? Maybe you have spent your free time helping a grandparent. How does understanding Jesus's sacrifice encourage you to put others first?

JESUS was not forced to die for our sins; He chose to die for us.

THE RESURRECTION

Have you ever been watching a TV show or movie but had to turn it off because it was time to leave or go to bed? Those moments are frustrating because we want to know how the story ends. Who wants *half* a story? Sometimes you might hear people say, "Jesus died for me, and that's the good news of the gospel." (The word **gospel** means "good news.") And although Jesus's dying for you and me is true and important, that's only *half* the story! Yes, Jesus died for your sins, but He didn't stay dead! Paul said,

> "For what I received I passed on to you as of first importance: that Christ died for our sins according to the Scriptures, that he was buried, that

> **Although Jesus's dying for you and me is true and important, that's only HALF the story!**

he was raised on the third day according to the Scriptures, and that he appeared to Cephas, and then to the Twelve. After that, he appeared to more than five hundred of the brothers and sisters at the same time." (1 Corinthians 15:3–6 NIV)

The gospel message isn't just "Jesus died for our sins." It is so important to remember that Jesus was resurrected; God raised Him to life again! If Jesus was not raised from the dead, then our faith isn't worth much of anything. Jesus's **resurrection** sets Him apart from every other sacrifice and every other person in history. So what is the resurrection, and what does it mean for you and me?

What's so special about resurrection?

Resurrection is different from someone being revived at the scene of an accident or in the hospital. When someone is *revived*, the person is dead for a very short time, but then medical workers make their heart start beating. With the help of special instruments, a person gains oxygen and begins to breathe on their own once more. They're revived, but that's not resurrection because that person will die again some other day.

So, yes, Jesus performed miracles and brought people such as Lazarus back to life, but Lazarus died again. Since the beginning of time, only Jesus has experienced resurrection. Resurrection involves the miraculous power of God to bring someone back from the dead and make them fully alive, never to die again!

What does Jesus's resurrected body look like?

Have you ever wondered if Jesus's resurrected body was like a ghost? The Bible teaches us that Jesus was raised in His own physical body. Jesus showed Himself to His disciples to prove it really was Him. Thomas wasn't convinced. So Jesus said, "Put your finger here; see my hands. Reach out your hand and put it into my side. Stop doubting and believe" (John 20:27 NIV). Thomas fell at Jesus's knees and believed Jesus really had been raised from the dead, not in a ghostly body but in His own physical body.

What does the resurrection mean for me now?

Jesus will never die again because God raised Jesus from the dead. What does this mean for you and me? First, we learn Jesus was "raised for our justification" (Romans 4:25). This means when Jesus rose from the dead, He changed our sinful record before God and made us acceptable in His sight. This is called righteousness; Jesus's perfection was given to us.

When Paul said we are justified, he was saying something very special. Being justified is not the same thing as being forgiven. Have you ever done something wrong and been forgiven by someone? If you were forgiven, that means the person doesn't have a grudge against you anymore. God forgives us, but He does more than that! Jesus gives us His perfect life record! That is justification. Justification is like going from deserving eternal in-school suspension to being the star student, rewarded with a pizza party! We are justified through the resurrection of Jesus.

No—Jesus cannot die again! When Jesus was raised from the dead, He was given a glorified body, the kind of body you will receive when He returns if you are His follower. In Revelation, the apostle John saw the resurrected Lord Jesus, and Jesus said, "Don't be afraid. I am the First and the Last, and the Living One. I was dead, but look—I am alive forever and ever" (Revelation 1:17–18). Jesus cannot die again. He is alive forever!

What will my resurrected body be like one day?

We have so many questions about our resurrected bodies. *How will they be different from our bodies right now? What will they be able to do?* Paul told us our new bodies will be immortal (they cannot die), powerful, and spiritual (1 Corinthians 15:35–58). The promise God made is that He will resurrect from the dead all who have trusted Jesus. We will get bodies then like Jesus has now! We will not get sick or suffer in any way. We will not be tempted to sin or hurt anyone or anything in all of creation. Our bodies will not grow tired or hungry. Doesn't that sound amazing?

TO THINK ABOUT:

What do you think it would've been like to be one of Jesus's disciples and to see Him standing in front of you, alive, after you watched Him die on the cross? Would you have quickly believed it was Him? Or would you have doubted, as Thomas did?

Can you think of three everyday ways you can show others that you believe Jesus really was resurrected?

The promise God made is that He will RESURRECT from the dead all who have trusted Jesus. We will get bodies then like Jesus has now!

THE HOLY SPIRIT

The third member of the Trinity is the Holy Spirit. Sometimes people will call Him "the Holy Ghost," but don't let that bother you! He's not a ghost floating around haunting people. In fact, Jesus called Him "the Comforter." More than that, the Holy Spirit convicts us of sin, guides us in making decisions, and empowers us to live for God's glory. This chapter is about the Holy Spirit—who He is, what He's like, and what He will do in your life.

After Jesus was raised from the dead, He went up into the clouds, back to heaven, and sat down on the throne at His Father's right hand. This is called the **ascension**. (To ascend means "to go up.") And He's still there today! Because Jesus is sitting, we know His work is complete.

Jesus calls the HOLY SPIRIT "the Comforter."

Fifty days after the resurrection, He and the Father sent the Holy Spirit into the Church at a festival called **Pentecost** (see Acts 2). This is exactly what Jesus had promised to do (see John 14:15–21). The Holy Spirit comes to dwell in the lives of all who trust in Jesus. Notice Jesus did not say the Holy Spirit *replaces* Him. Instead, the Holy Spirit *reveals* the ways of Jesus to us (see John 16:7–15).

Is the Holy Spirit an it or a He?

As the third member of the Trinity, the Holy Spirit is not an *it*; He is a person. And because the Holy Spirit is a person, that means He is not an impersonal force. Not only does He relate to the Father and the Son, but He also uniquely relates to every one of God's children.

The Holy Spirit is not like food, toys, or clothing that we simply go to a store to get. Instead, He comes into our lives on His own timetable, and when He does, it is always because someone has proclaimed the gospel of Jesus to us. The Holy Spirit helps us see our great need for Jesus and the salvation He brings. He convicts us of sin and gives us the gift of repentance. **Repentance** means to come to agree with God about where we have failed and then turn toward following God and away from our sin. When the Holy Spirit comes into your life, He magnifies Jesus and gives you a love for the Church and a desire for others to come to faith too.

The Holy Spirit does an enormous amount of work in us throughout our lives. For one, He *guides* us. Jesus said, "But when he, the Spirit of truth, comes, he will *guide* you into all the truth" (John 16:13 NIV). The Holy Spirit wants to see you growing in your faith. Because He dwells in you as you follow Jesus, He is always going to lead you toward the truth.

The Holy Spirit does the work of **conviction**. Conviction has to do with making the truth known. The Bible says God is light, meaning He exposes the darkness in the world and in our own hearts. The Holy Spirit lets us know when we're in the wrong, when we sin against God, ourselves, and other people. But He doesn't just leave us on our own once we realize we've sinned. He also *empowers* us to live the Christian life!

- **The Holy Spirit empowers us to serve the Church.** In 1 Corinthians 12:4–11, we learn we are empowered to serve the Church. This is because Jesus is the head of the Church (Colossians 1:18) and cares deeply for its well-being. Paul also told us we must remember that of all the things the Holy Spirit does, the most important is to help us love one another. It's not much use if we're gifted to do something wonderful but don't actually love others (1 Corinthians 13:1).

- **The Holy Spirit empowers us to share the gospel.** Jesus told us that the Holy Spirit empowers us to share the gospel's good news with others! This means when you're talking to your friends about Jesus, you are not on your own, and you don't have to feel pressure to always have all the answers. When talking about our faith, some things can't be explained the way we would like. But we do not have to fear or be ashamed of talking about Jesus. Instead, the Holy Spirit empowers us to be bold and to lovingly invite others to follow Jesus too.

- **The Holy Spirit empowers us to pray.** The Holy Spirit helps us remain in an ongoing relationship with God through prayer. We are encouraged to seek the gifts of the Holy Spirit (1 Corinthians 14:1). This means we are to pray often about how He would empower us to best serve other followers of Jesus around us.

How does the Holy Spirit comfort me?

We know God hears us because He makes this promise in His Word. For example, Psalm 116 says, "I love the LORD, for he heard my voice; he heard my cry for mercy. Because he turned his ear to me, I will call on him as long as I live" (vv.1–2 NIV). Remember, as a follower of Jesus, you are in an ongoing relationship with God because of the gift of the Holy Spirit. Paul wrote, "Because you are his sons [and daughters], God sent the Spirit of his Son into our hearts, the Spirit who calls out, '*Abba*, Father'" (Galatians 4:6 NIV). The word **Abba** means "Daddy." The Holy Spirit doesn't come and go but remains with you always; He comforts you by always leading you back to a tender relationship with your heavenly Father.

TO THINK ABOUT:

Think about the most memorable gift you've ever received. What made it special? Do you still have it? Now think about the gift of the Holy Spirit. What makes His presence so special? How do you feel about His promise to always be with you?

The
HOLY SPIRIT
doesn't come and
go but remains
with you
always.

91

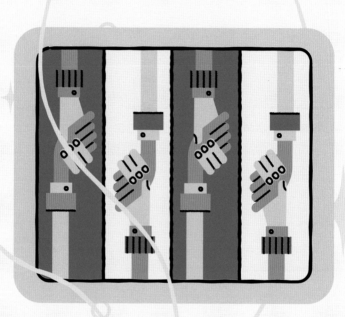

THE CHURCH

When you were little, you might have thought a church was nothing more than a building with a cross on it. But a church has little to do with the building and everything to do with the people.

In the first-century world (the time of the New Testament), the word **ecclesia** (pronounced ekk-lay-see-uh) was used for church. Ecclesia simply means "gathering." So an ecclesia of athletes might be getting ready to play a game or an ecclesia of actors is outside the theater talking about the play they will perform. And an ecclesia of Christians makes a church.

Jesus said, "I will build my church" (Matthew 16:18). This means *Jesus* is the founder and builder of the ecclesia of people who have come together in His name.

> **JESUS is the founder and builder of the ecclesia of people who have come together in His name.**

The Church belongs to Jesus, not your pastor or anyone else. Jesus died for the Church. Jesus gave the Holy Spirit to the Church. Jesus is returning one day for the Church. Jesus loves the Church! Notice we haven't even mentioned "church buildings"! This is because the Church Jesus is building is always *people*. We gather in church buildings, houses, or anywhere in Jesus's name.

What makes a church?

A group of Christians sitting in a room doesn't automatically make a church. The Bible tells us a few things need to be put in place and consistently practiced for a gathering of Christians to be recognized as a church family. The group must have qualified leadership, preach the gospel, and offer what's called the sacraments (or ordinances)—baptism and communion.

Qualified church leadership is made up of elders and deacons. These leaders are called to be people who, among other things, tell the truth, can teach others, are friendly and welcoming to guests, and are self-controlled, respectable, and gentle (1 Timothy 3 and Titus 1). These leaders are responsible for teaching clearly from the Bible and caring for the church family. They help meet the needs of others and pray for people. They are also to actively train other leaders to come and help in the work of the ministry (Ephesians 4:11–12).

What's so important about the Church?

Jesus gives the Holy Spirit to the churches He builds, and one thing Jesus said the Holy Spirit would do is glorify Him (John 16:14). The Holy Spirit loves to magnify Jesus and see Him lifted up. One key way the Church consistently lifts up Jesus is by faithfully proclaiming the gospel's good news: *Jesus, the King of Israel, is the*

Savior of the world! And this is super important for you to remember—the gospel message is not only what we share with unbelievers but also what followers of Jesus need to hear again and again so we won't forget about God's grace and love. You'll never outgrow your need to hear the good news! Just like it would be impossible for you to grow strong and healthy eating only junk food, so it is with following Jesus. To grow in your walk with Him, you need the vitamins of the faith: going to church, being part of the community, showing up to be encouraged and to encourage others, praying together, and being held accountable.

What are the sacraments?

The word **sacrament** means "sacred mystery." The word *mystery* is helpful because that's really what the sacraments are; they are God's beautiful, creative ways of connecting with and reminding us of Jesus and the gospel message. The sacraments of the Church are baptism and communion. Baptism represents several things. Here are three: First, it is a picture of washing away sin.

Second, it is a picture of being plunged into a life with the Trinity. Third, it is about identifying with all followers of Jesus, kind of like putting on a uniform. Communion represents important parts of our faith too. When Christians take communion, the broken bread represents Jesus's body, which was beaten and crucified, and the wine or juice represents His blood, 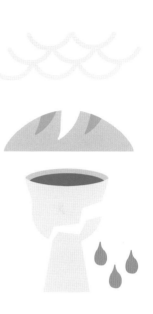 which was given for us. It is also a picture of our unity with Christ and with His body—the Church—all over the world.

Churches all over the world practice baptism and communion in different ways. Perhaps you could ask a leader at your church to explain to you what your church believes about baptism and communion.

What if I don't want to go to church?

This question brings up all kinds of feelings, and that is okay! The Bible tells us the importance of "not giving up meeting together" (Hebrews 10:25 NIV). In other words, go to church, gather with the people, and worship God. But sometimes we are tired, don't like the people, or are just bored and would rather do something else. Pastors, Sunday school teachers, and theologians feel this way from time to time, and that's entirely normal. We are still in our earthly bodies with all kinds of weaknesses and distractions. Paul said we battle the flesh and the spirit. So what are we to do when we just don't feel like going to church? What can help us get back on track?

First, we remember that to be a disciple of Jesus means we need to be disciplined; we will have to challenge ourselves to grow. Second, we remember that Jesus Himself made worshiping with God's people part of His custom. If it was a priority for Jesus to gather with the people of God, then it needs to be our priority too, regardless of how we feel on a particular day. Third, we remind ourselves of the times we learned something from Scripture or experienced the joy of connecting with a friend or serving someone else. We can allow that memory to give our souls a jump start. Finally, we remember that our salvation is not based on our perfect church attendance, but rather on the resurrection of Jesus. He forgave our sins, longs for a closer relationship with us, and has asked us to gather in His name.

TO **THINK** ABOUT:

Make a list of all the important things you do at church. You might include singing worship songs, praying, hearing a Bible lesson or sermon, enjoying time with your friends.

Do each of those activities make you closer to God? How are they different when you do them on your own? How does it feel to know that people all over the world are gathering in churches and worshiping God by doing many of the same things? You are part of God's big, big Church!

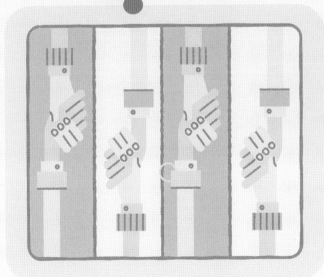

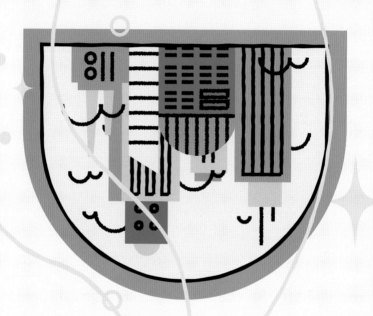

HEAVEN ON EARTH

What comes to mind when you think about heaven? One popular image people have is of fat babies with wings sitting around on big puffy clouds with halos floating overhead as they play the harp forever. If that sounds silly, weird, or just plain terrible, don't worry. It's completely wrong! The Bible uses the phrase "new heavens and a new earth" (Isaiah 65:17; Revelation 21:5) to describe the place He is preparing for us after our time on this earth as it is right now. The life to come in heaven is not a repeat of this life! Yes, you'll be you, and I'll be me, and this world will be this world, but everything, absolutely everything, will be made totally new, completely perfect!

So we'll have to use our imaginations, guided by the Bible, to think about heaven.

> The life to come in HEAVEN is not a repeat of this life!

Where is heaven?

Heaven is the unique, special, extraordinary living place of God. Yes, a *place*! Here's a mystery. Remember, at the beginning of this book we discussed that God is omnipresent—He is everywhere at all times. There is no place God does not inhabit. At the same time, the Bible teaches that God's presence also dwells uniquely in a place called heaven. So heaven is a place, but it's not the kind of place you can point to or find on a map.

Heaven is the place where God is crowned King and reigns from His royal throne. Heaven is the place where God is worshiped by angels, surrounded by majestic creatures, and glorified, celebrated, and praised for who He is and all He has done. Heaven is the place where the spirits of all Christians who have died now live. This means my daddy, William, is in the presence of God alongside Abraham, Moses, Mary, and Peter. And God's not finished yet! Heaven is coming to earth!

What is the new heavens and new earth, and where is God going to build it?

The Bible tells us God is ever-committed to restoring and healing His creation, which He originally called "good" (Genesis 1:31). Peter told us that "the day of the Lord will come like a thief, and then the heavens will pass away with a roar, and the heavenly bodies will be burned up and dissolved, and the earth and the works that are done on it will be exposed" (2 Peter 3:10 ESV). The "burning" here is like a **purifying** fire—a fire that puts away all sin, death, decay, and destruction that corrupted God's world. It's not a fire that will destroy His world entirely.

Hebrews 13:14 says, "Here we have no lasting city, but we seek the city that is to come" (ESV). Some interpret this verse to teach a form of escapism; that is, this world is useless, and so we should simply wait on heaven. But the Bible is not saying, "God is going to throw this whole creation in a landfill somewhere and make an entirely new creation!" Rather, it is saying the cities and places we live in *now* will not always be this way! One day there will be no more violence, hunger, or reason to lock our doors. God is going to renew this world, and we look forward to living in that city. Heaven is where God is reigning over all creation with His people without the threat of sin or the consequences that come with rebellion against God.

What will we do in heaven?

The Bible teaches that heaven will last for eternity; that is, forever. So what will we *do* day after day for forever? Some people imagine heaven being like a church worship service where we sing and sing and sing and sing and sing forever. We most certainly will sing to the glory of God; all creation will join in, and it will be glorious! We will celebrate the Father, Son, and Holy Spirit and all God has done to redeem His creation. But in the new heavens and earth, we'll have more to do than just sing.

The Bible tells us we will be working, eating, drinking, and resting.

It might sound odd to have *work* as one of the things we'll be doing in heaven. Isn't work the result of sin? It isn't! Remember that when God created Adam and Eve, He placed them in the garden of Eden to work (Genesis 2:15). After sin entered creation, work (like everything else) fell under the curse and became very hard. Yet the apostle John told us that, in heaven, God's "servants will serve him" (Revelation 22:3 NIV). This means our work in the new heavens and new earth is out from under the curse, completely redeemed! The Bible doesn't tell us exactly what our work will be, but we know it will be rewarding, satisfying, exciting, and glorifying to God.

Although we will work in heaven, we will *rest* from all our work too (Revelation 14:13). In the new heavens and new earth, we will have all eternity to rest. We will be refreshed in every way as we live in the presence of God forever.

TO **THINK** ABOUT:

Make a list of your least favorite, hardest things in life. Maybe it's failing a test in class, being sick, or having to say goodbye to someone you love. Take a minute to imagine being in heaven, where none of those negative things will ever exist. Now thank God for creating a wonderful forever home for us! What are you most looking forward to doing in heaven?

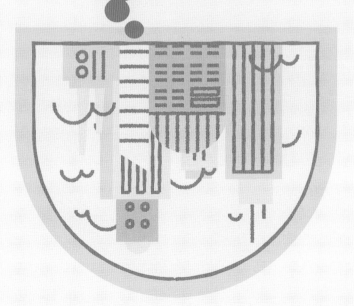

DON'T STOP THINKING

You made it! You're at the end of our journey through *Thinking About God*! How did you do? Did you find some answers to your questions? Maybe a few more questions were sparked? We began with a warm welcome to the world of theology, and I hope you found yourself feeling at home as you thought about God, His Word, this world, and your own faith. Let's summarize what we covered.

First, we studied the Trinity; the Father, Son, and Holy Spirit are three persons and yet one being. All theology begins with God, not creation, sin, or anything else. We learned about the incommunicable attributes of God (omnipresence, omniscience, omnipotence) and the noetic effects of sin (how sin affects our thinking).

 We also thought about God's power to create *ex nihilo* (out of nothing).

Next time you set out to create something in art class, remind yourself that God needed zero materials to make all that you see!

Then we studied the *imago dei*—the image of God in human beings. Everyone you see today is uniquely made in the image of God.

In chapter 5 we thought about sin and the Fall. Take time to pray and ask God for His forgiveness of your sins.

From there we looked into our need for leadership (prophets, priests, and kings) in a fallen world. Think about all the people who lead you and how you can pray for God to guide them.

Chapter 7 answered questions about what Jesus was like and the significance of His miracles. Perhaps you know someone who is sick and needs Jesus's healing!

In chapter 8 we thought about the atonement with an emphasis on the Passover, justification, and pro-pitiation. If you follow Jesus, your sins are forgiven, and God finds no fault, nothing wrong with you!

Then we studied the importance of Jesus's resurrection from the dead and what that means for us. You've been invited to be part of God's plan to bring an entirely new way of living into this world.

After the resurrection, the Holy Spirit was sent into the lives of those who trusted Jesus. Remember: if you follow Jesus, His Spirit is always leading, guiding, and empowering you.

In chapter 11 we talked about how God not only brings us into a relationship with

Himself, but He also brings us into His family, the Church. And He gives His Church the gift of building each other up in love.

Finally, we took time to think about the new heavens and new earth, the hope of all followers of Jesus.

You now know so many new things about God! Take this knowledge and let it change the way you read the Bible, the way you treat people, and the way you live. The point of all theology is to bring us to what's called **doxology**, which is an expression of praise to God. It's what happens when we begin to get our minds around who God is and what He has done for us. Right thinking leads to right living, which leads to glorifying our God for who He is and all He has done!

WORDS TO KNOW

1. **Apostles**. Means "sent ones." In the New Testament, the apostles were the followers of Jesus who were eyewitnesses of His resurrection and then sent by Him to preach the gospel. Later in the history of the Church, apostles referred to others being sent to share the gospel.

2. **Ascension**. When Jesus was taken up to heaven in front of eyewitnesses after His resurrection.

3. **Aseity.** Means that God proceeds from His own self.

4. **Atonement**. Means "to cover" and references the fact that Jesus's blood "covers" all our sins.

5. **Attributes of God**. The characteristics or traits belonging to God.

6. **Baptism**. A sacrament that points to Jesus and means "to be submerged." When we see baptism in worship, a person is sometimes submerged under the water. It is a picture of the life (someone standing in the water), death (someone going under

the water), and resurrection (someone coming back out of the water) of Jesus.

7. **Christology**. The study of the person and work of Jesus Christ.

8. **Communicable attributes of God**. The characteristics of God that He shares with humans.

9. **Communion**. The sacrament of bread and wine or juice used in worship services, reminding Christians of Jesus's body that was crucified and the blood He shed for the forgiveness of our sins.

10. **Conviction**. To feel responsible for sin.

11. **Creation**. All that exists. All that is seen and unseen, made by God and for God.

12. **Creator**. God as the originator and maker of all things.

13. **Doxology**. An expression of praise to God.

14. **Ex nihilo**. Means "out of nothing." When God created all things, there were no existing materials for Him to use. He supernaturally made everything out of nothing.

15. **Fall**. When Eve and then Adam ate the forbidden fruit in the garden and fell into sin.

16. **General revelation**. The truths about God that can be understood by observing the natural world.

17. **Gospel**. The good news of salvation found only in Jesus Christ.

18. **Incommunicable attributes of God**. The attributes of God that He does not share with anything or anyone else in all creation.

19. **Justification**. God's declaration that someone is righteous before Him.

20. **Messiah**. The anointed, sacred rescuer of God's people.

21. **Miracle**. An event in which God suspends the laws of nature to bring about His will on the earth.

22. **Noetic**. Having to do with the mind.

23. **Omnipotence**. The incommunicable attribute of God having unlimited power.

24. **Omnipresence**. The incommunicable attribute of God being in all places at all times.

25. **Omniscient**. The incommunicable attribute of God having knowledge of everything.

26. **Passover**. The night of the Exodus when God's people sacrificed lambs and painted their door-frames with their blood, causing God's judgment to pass over His people as He judged Egypt and set the Hebrews free.

27. **Pentecost**. Originally a festival held by the Jewish people to celebrate the grain harvest. In the book of Acts, it was at this festival when the people of God received the Holy Spirit.

28. **Prayer**. Communicating with God by speaking to Him or patiently pausing to listen with our hearts to what the Holy Spirit might be saying.

29. **Prophets**. Those who speak from God's perspective.

30. **Propitiation**. The wrath-averting sacrifice of Jesus.

31. **Redemption**. Christ's work to save God's people from both sin and the consequences of sin.

32. **Repentance**. To change your mind and actions about sin and turn to God for forgiveness.

33. **Restoration**. When God will make all things new.

34. **Resurrection**. The physical, bodily raising of Jesus (and one day all followers of Jesus) from the dead, now with a glorified body, unable to sin, harm, or be corrupted.

35. **Righteousness**. Being made morally right or upright before God.

36. **Sacraments**. The practices of being baptized in water and receiving communion, both reminding the believer of God's faithfulness to save.

37. **Savior**. Jesus, whose name means "the Lord saves." Our sin against God requires that we be rescued (or "saved") from the consequences of sin (eternal separation from God).

38. **Sin**. Thoughts, words, and actions that rebel against God's will.

39. **Special revelation**. When God reveals Himself to a person or people through visions, dreams,

prophets, angels, Jesus Christ, the Scriptures, or the Holy Spirit.

40. **Theology**. A combination of two Greek words: *theos* meaning "God," and *logos* meaning "word," "reason," or "logic." Theology is thinking about God.

41. **Transfiguration**. When Jesus became radiant with the glory of God on the mountaintop.

42. **Trinity**. One God existing as three persons—the Father, Son, and Holy Spirit.